MASTERPIXELS
AMAZING WILDLIFE

120 SECRET COLORING PATTERNS

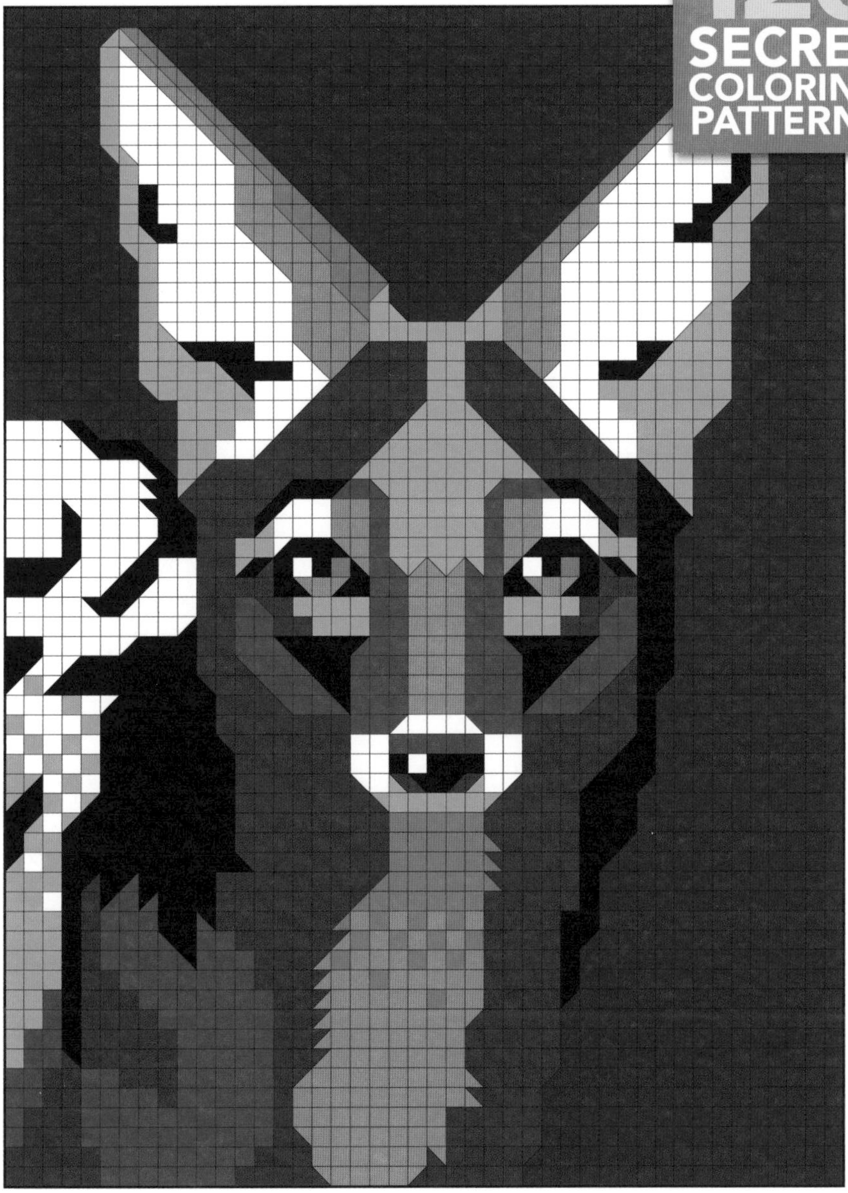

DIEGO JOURDAN PEREIRA

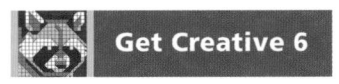

Get Creative 6

NEW YORK

MASTERPIXELS AMAZING WILDLIFE

1	Yellow
2	Deep Yellow
3	Gold
4	Orange
5	Orange Red
6	Red
7	Purple
8	Pink
9	Peach
10	Light Violet
11	Violet
12	Violet Blue
13	Blue
14	Light Blue
15	Indigo Blue
16	Yellow Green
17	Green
18	Grass Green
19	Dark Green
20	Sienna Brown
21	Dark Red
22	Dark Brown
23	Black

BEFORE

AFTER

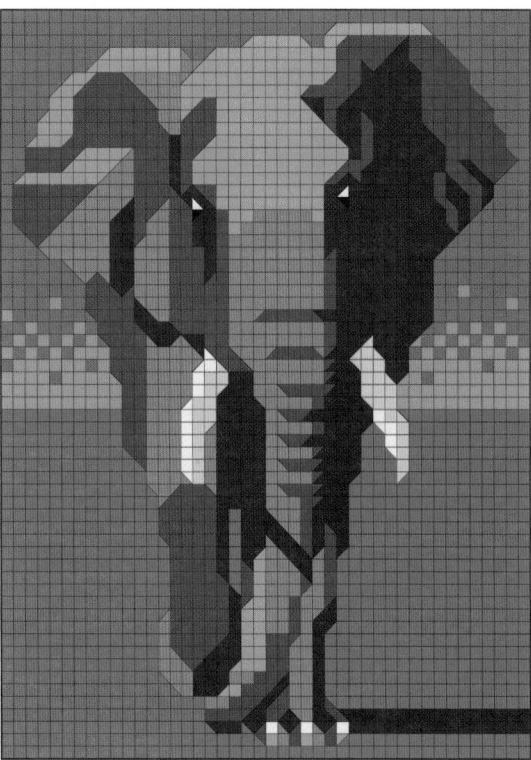

"The painter's mind is a copy of the divine mind, since it operates freely in creating the many kinds of animals, plants, fruits, landscapes, countrysides, ruins, and awe-inspiring places."
—Leonardo da Vinci

Paint-by-number can be traced back to the famous painter Leonardo da Vinci, who assigned numbered sections to his paintings for assistants to fill, which he later went over with oil paints. His idea was picked up centuries later for paint-by-number kits beloved by hobbyists. My childhood home had one such picture, a German shepherd my dad painted, still in my mind when I illustrated my first color-by-number volumes, eventually leading me to the book you're holding in your hands. Its puzzles will keep you guessing which creatures will come to life, providing hours of fun. It's also my hope that once revealed, they will bring you the same love for nature I felt while designing them. Enjoy!

—Diego Jourdan Pereira

REVEALING THE SECRET MASTERPIECES

Like other color-by-number books, this one's puzzles contain numbered areas to fill with corresponding colors from the provided palette key at left to reveal an image, but unlike vintage color-by-number, the ones here have been divided with a grid pattern that requires sharp concentration to crack each puzzle. The final masterpieces won't be revealed unless you color every pixel (except the white ones, leave those blank). When in doubt, you can always flip to the back of the book, where color answer keys provide guidance.

PUZZLE 1

PUZZLE 2

PUZZLE 3

PUZZLE 4

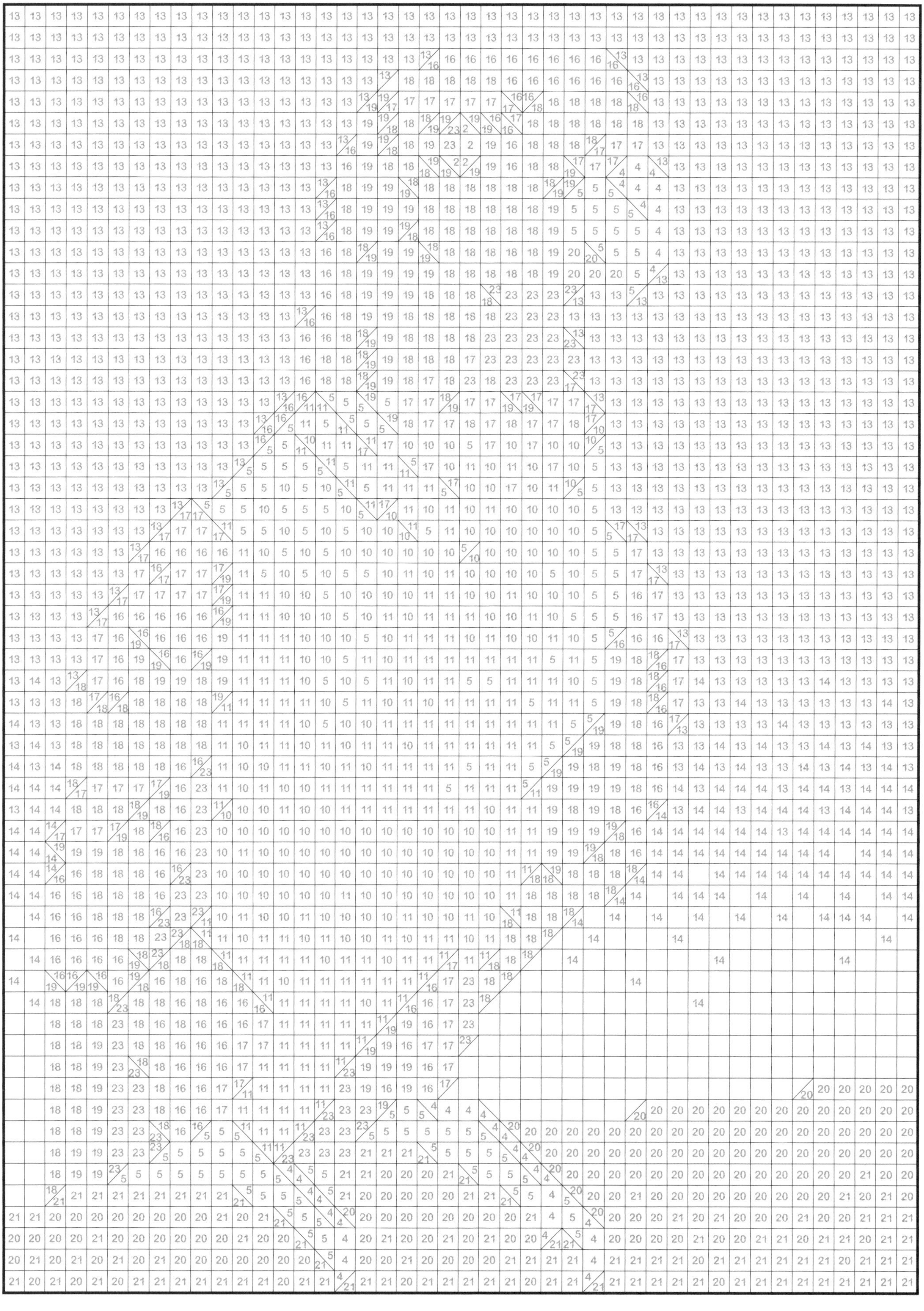

PUZZLE 5

PUZZLE 6

PUZZLE 8

PUZZLE 10

PUZZLE 12

PUZZLE 13

PUZZLE 14

PUZZLE 15

PUZZLE 16

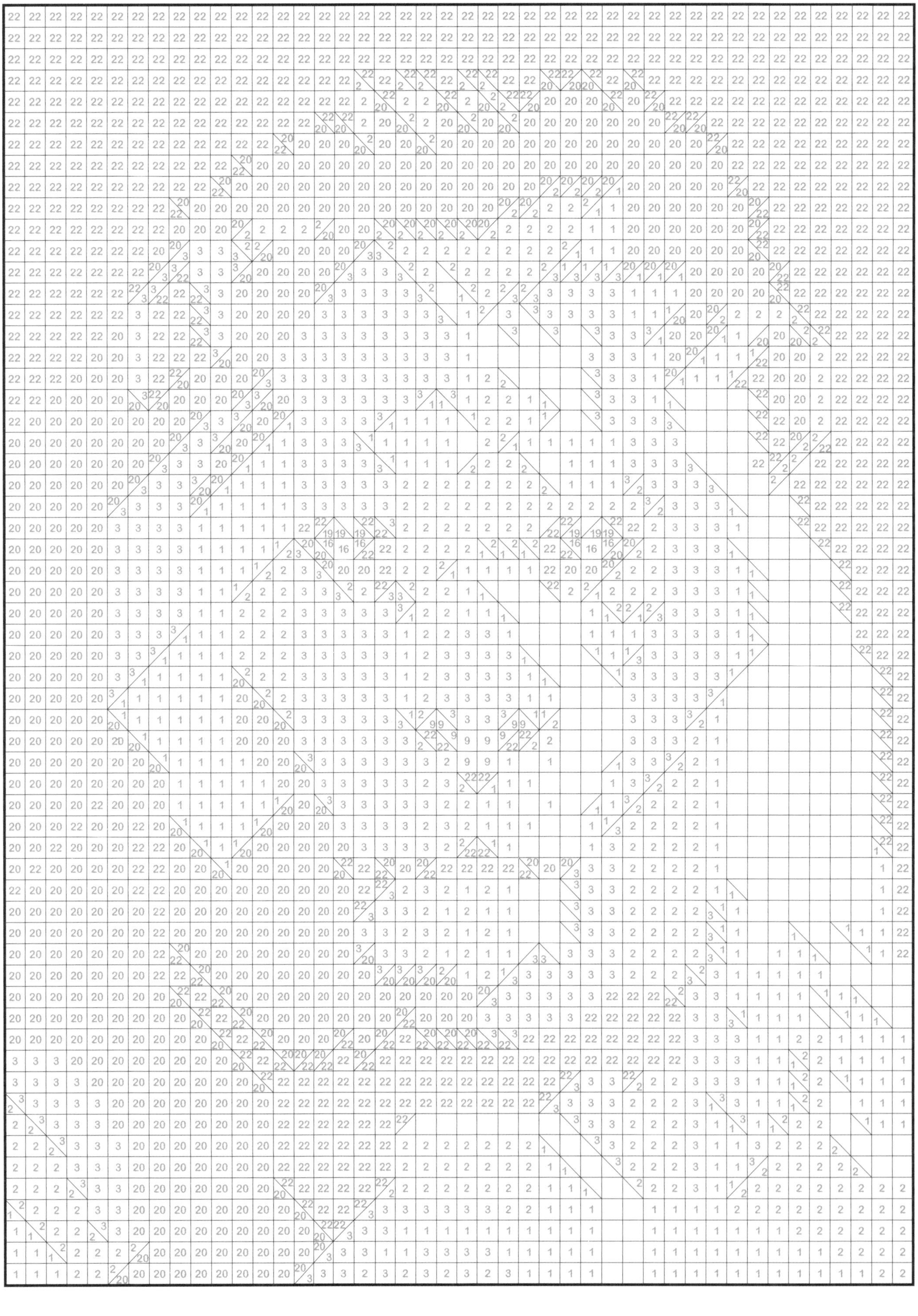

PUZZLE 17

PUZZLE 18

PUZZLE 19

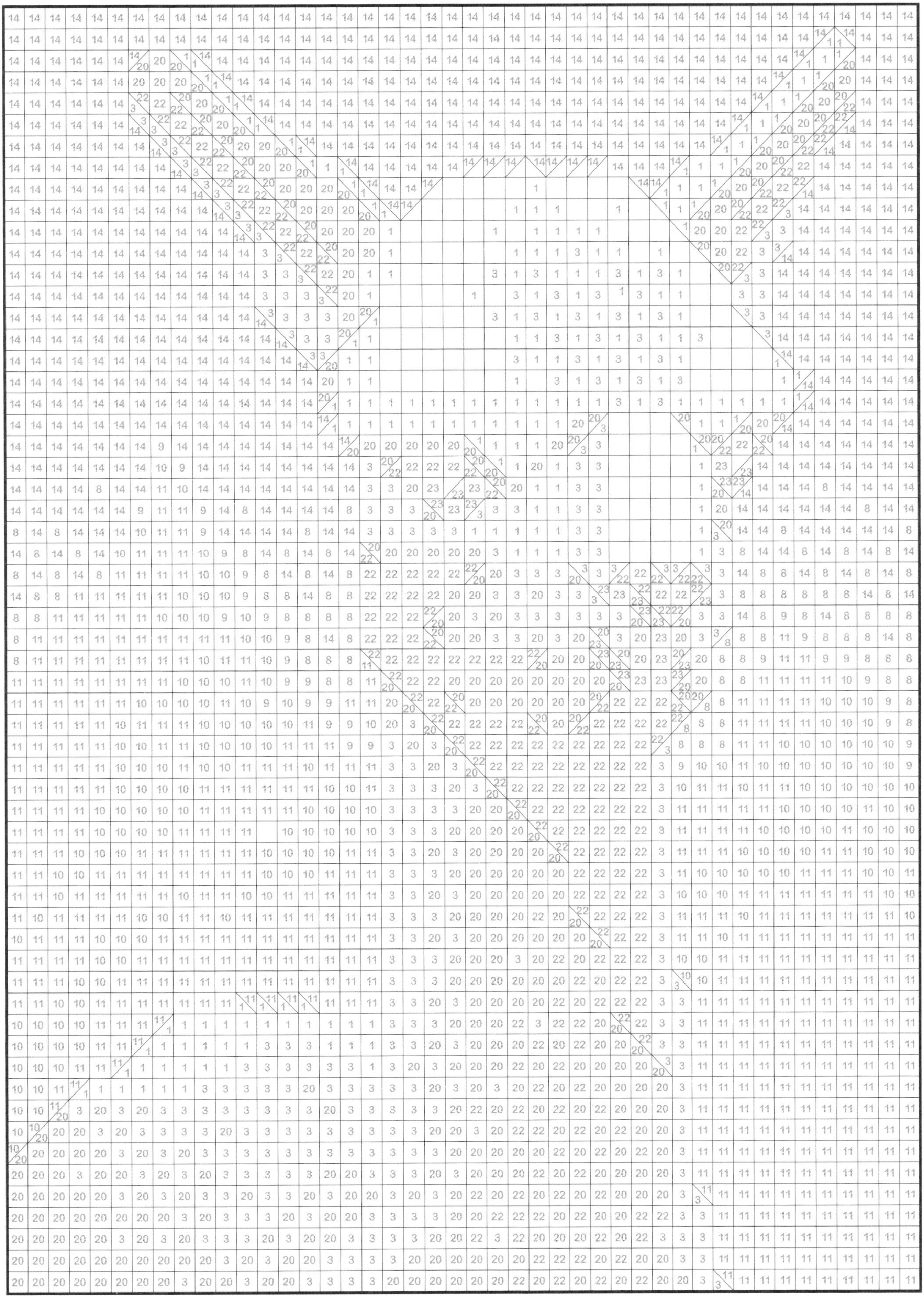

PUZZLE 21

PUZZLE 22

PUZZLE 23

PUZZLE 24

PUZZLE 25

PUZZLE 26

PUZZLE 27

PUZZLE 28

PUZZLE 29

PUZZLE 30

PUZZLE 32

PUZZLE 33

PUZZLE 34

PUZZLE 35

PUZZLE 36

PUZZLE 37

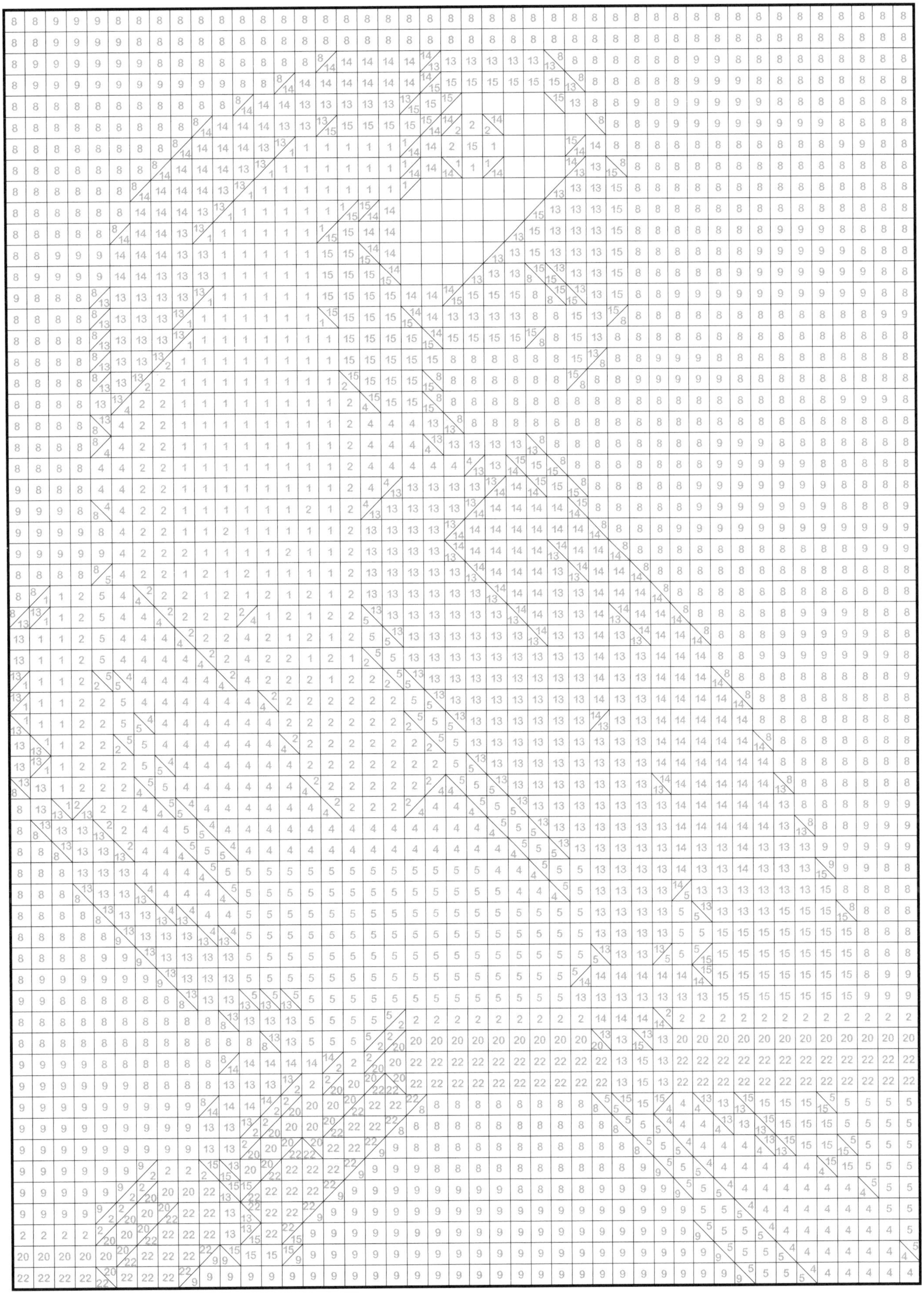

PUZZLE 38

PUZZLE 39

PUZZLE 40

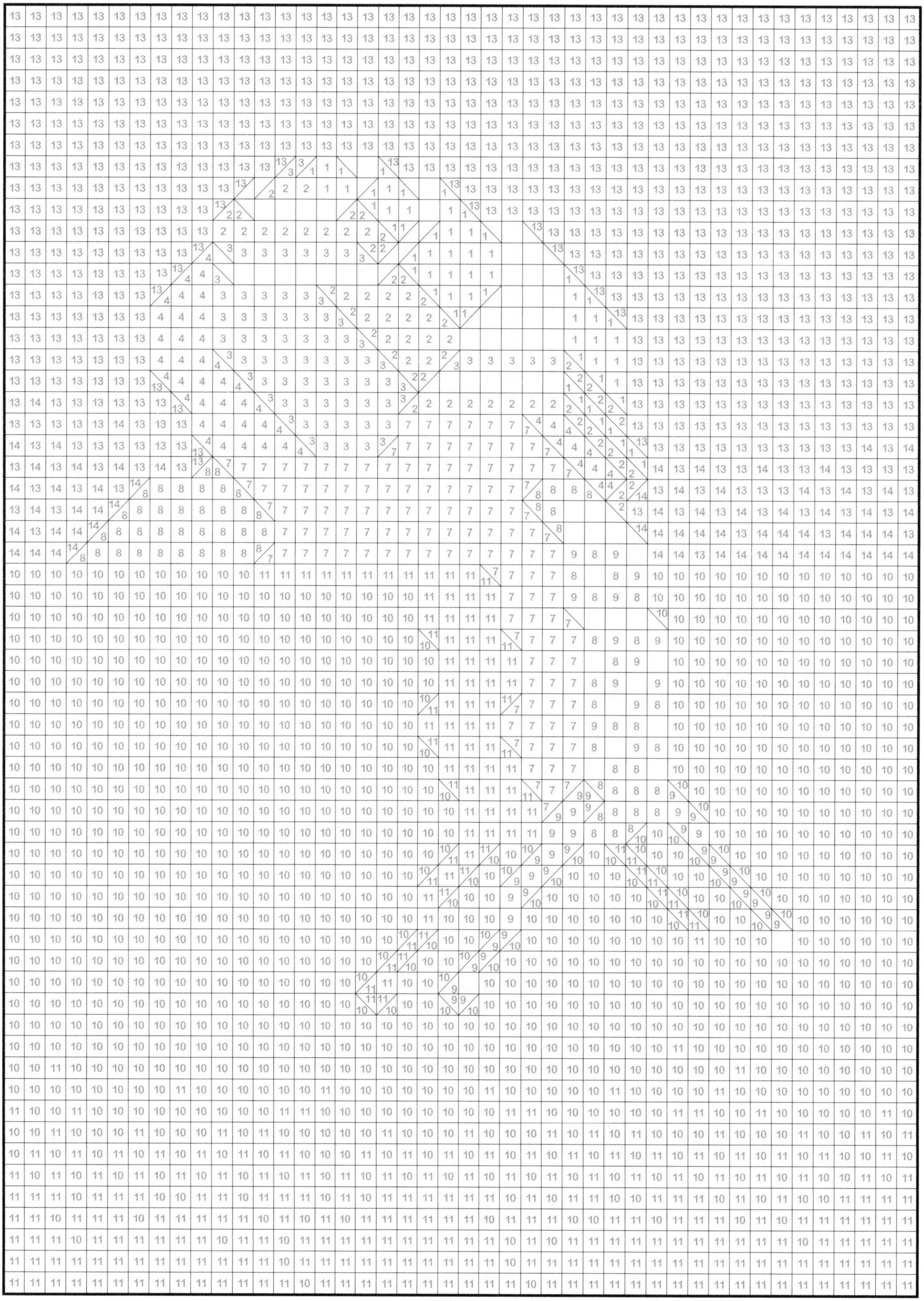

PUZZLE 41

PUZZLE 42

PUZZLE 44

PUZZLE 45

PUZZLE 46

PUZZLE 47

PUZZLE 48

PUZZLE 49

PUZZLE 50

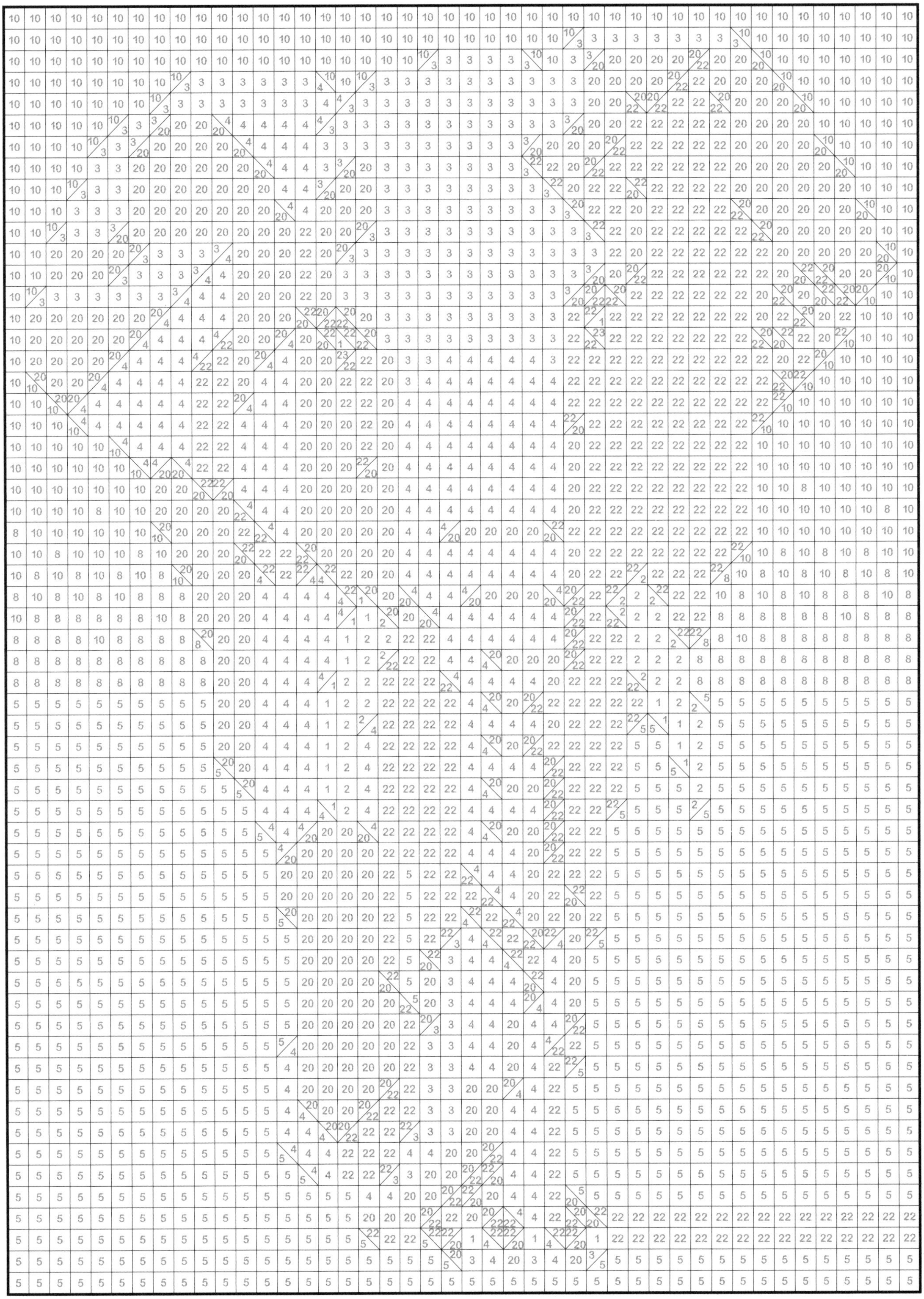

PUZZLE 51

PUZZLE 52

PUZZLE 53

PUZZLE 54

PUZZLE 55

PUZZLE 56

PUZZLE 57

PUZZLE 58

PUZZLE 59

PUZZLE 60

PUZZLE 61

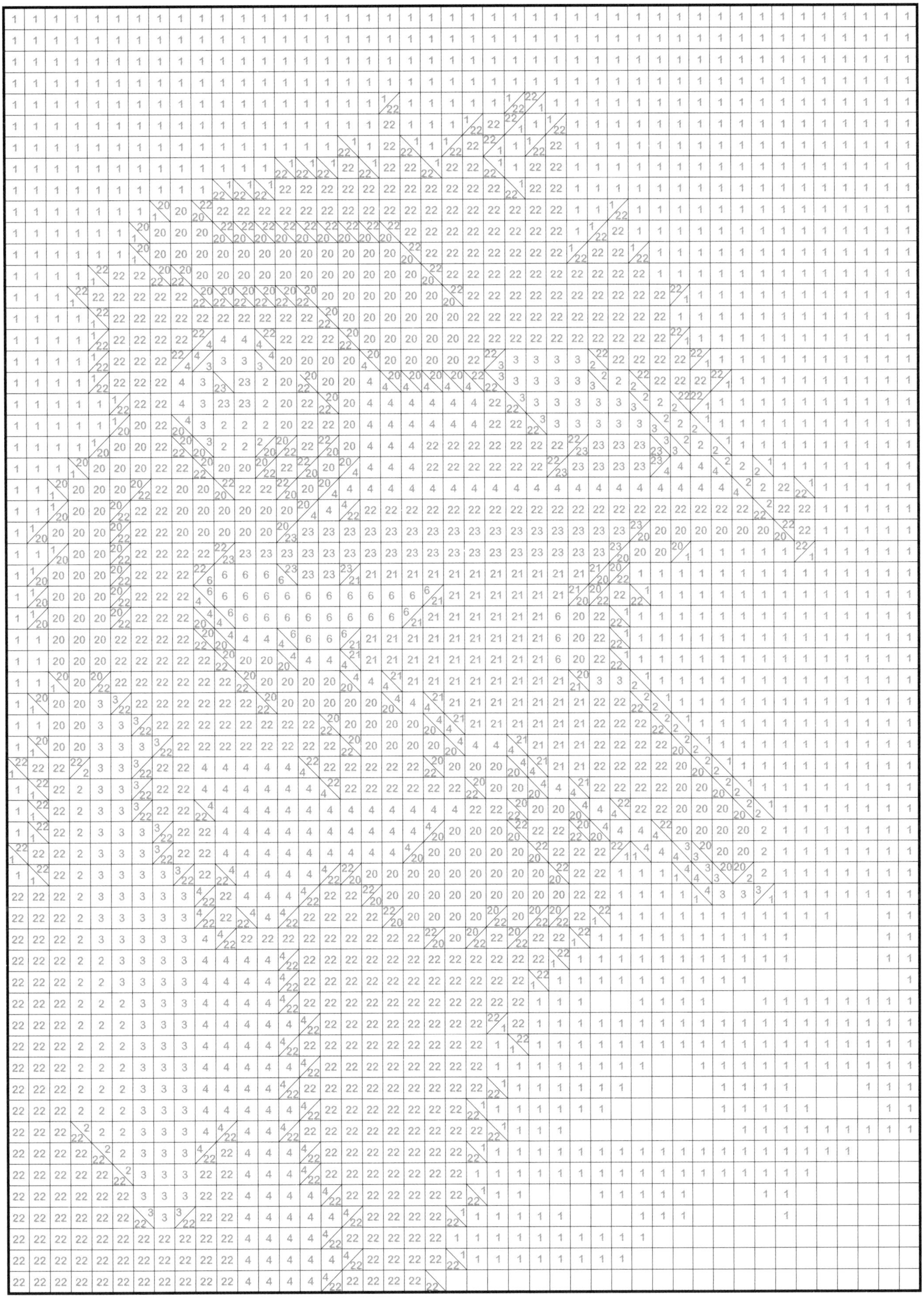

PUZZLE 62

PUZZLE 63

PUZZLE 65

PUZZLE 66

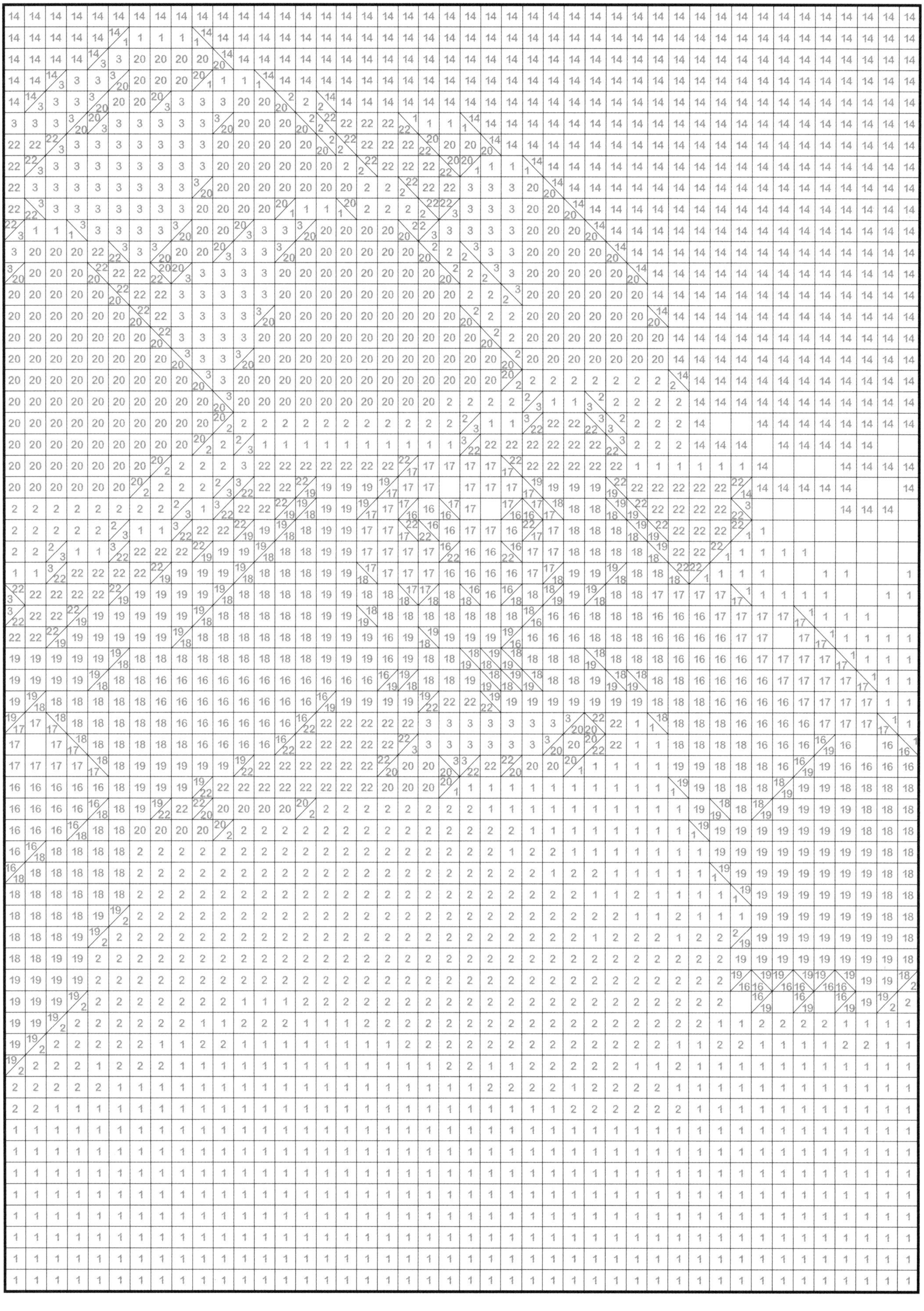

PUZZLE 67

PUZZLE 68

PUZZLE 69

PUZZLE 71

PUZZLE 72

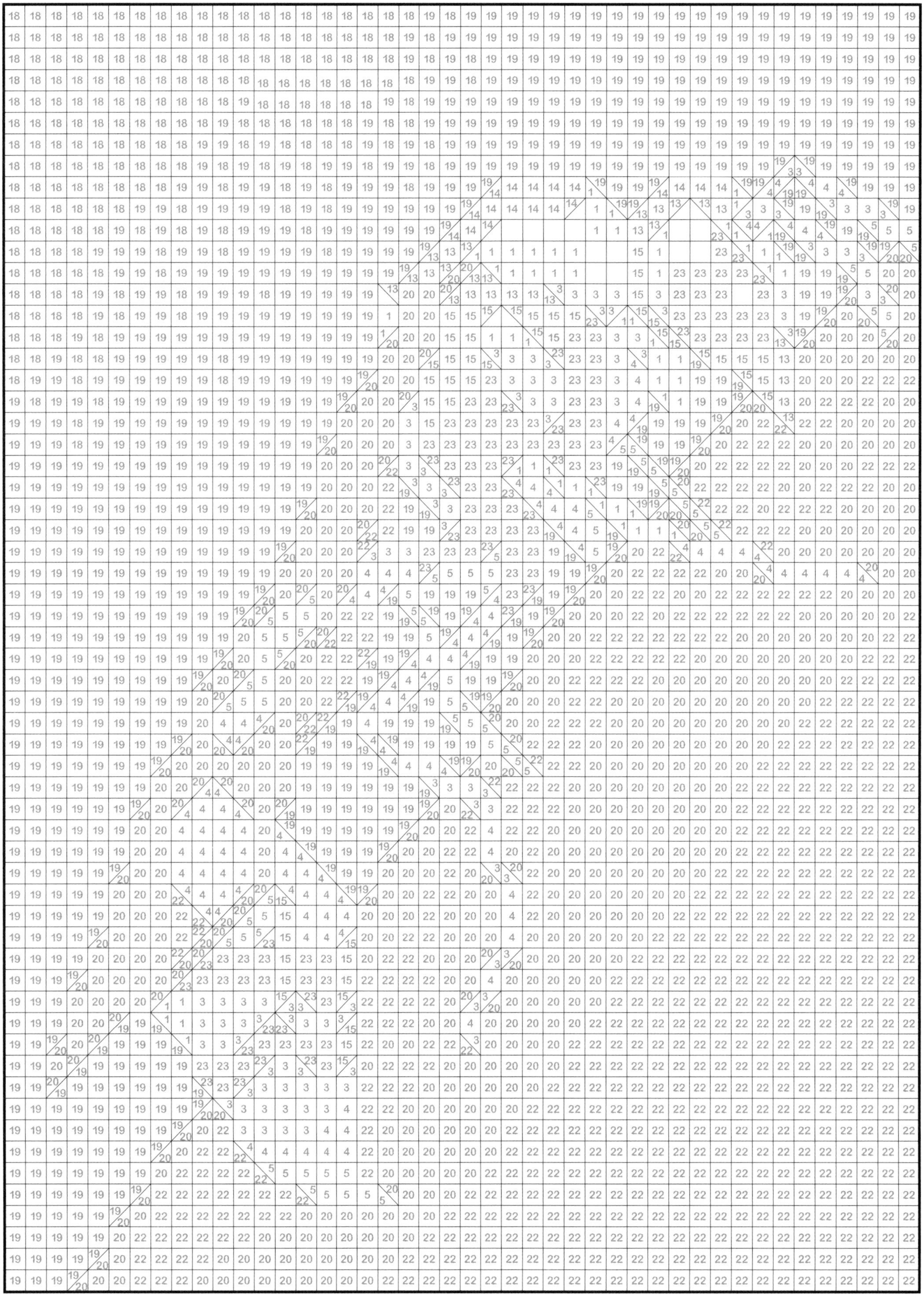

PUZZLE 73

PUZZLE 74

PUZZLE 75

PUZZLE 76

PUZZLE 77

PUZZLE 78

PUZZLE 79

PUZZLE 80

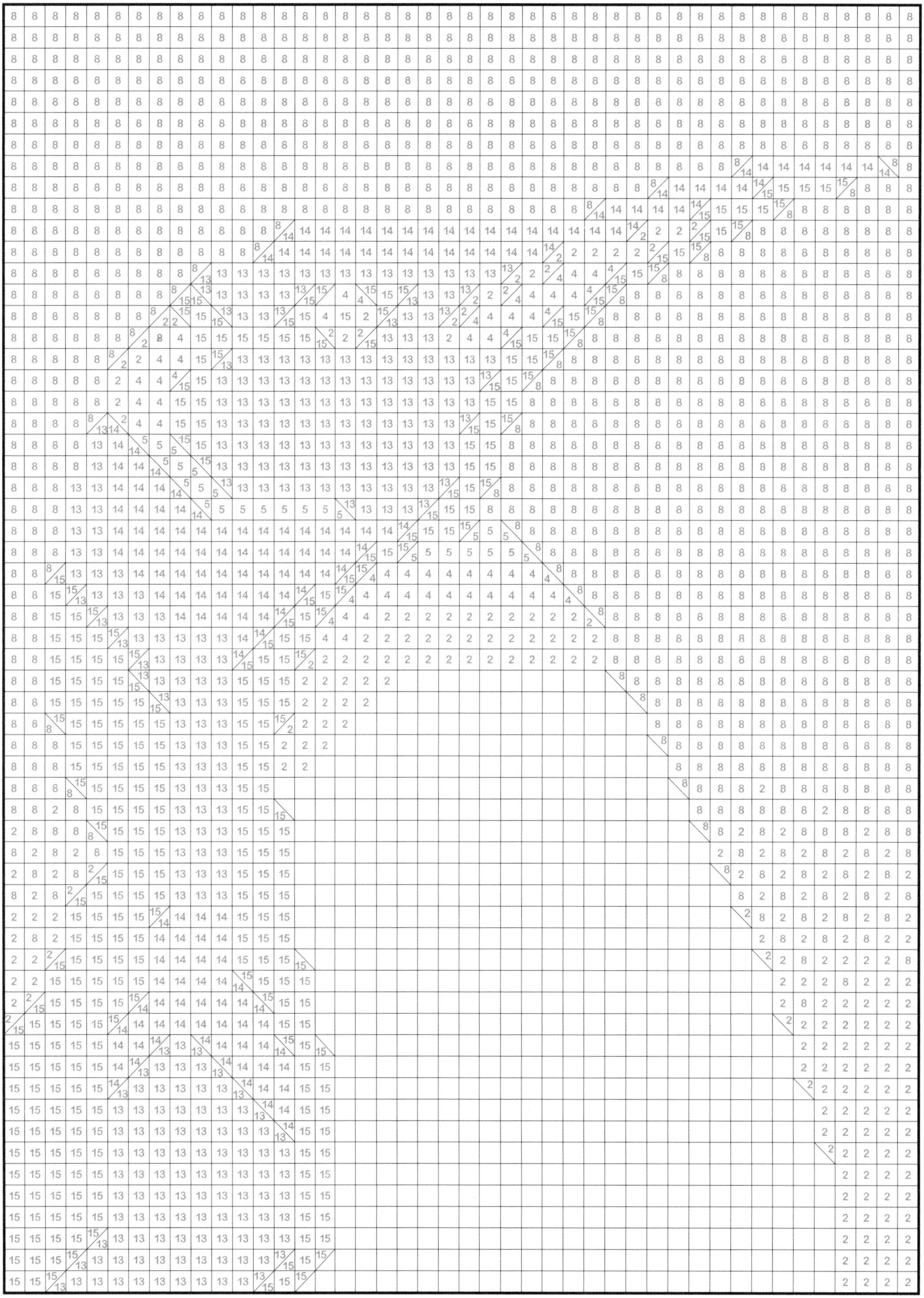

PUZZLE 81

PUZZLE 82

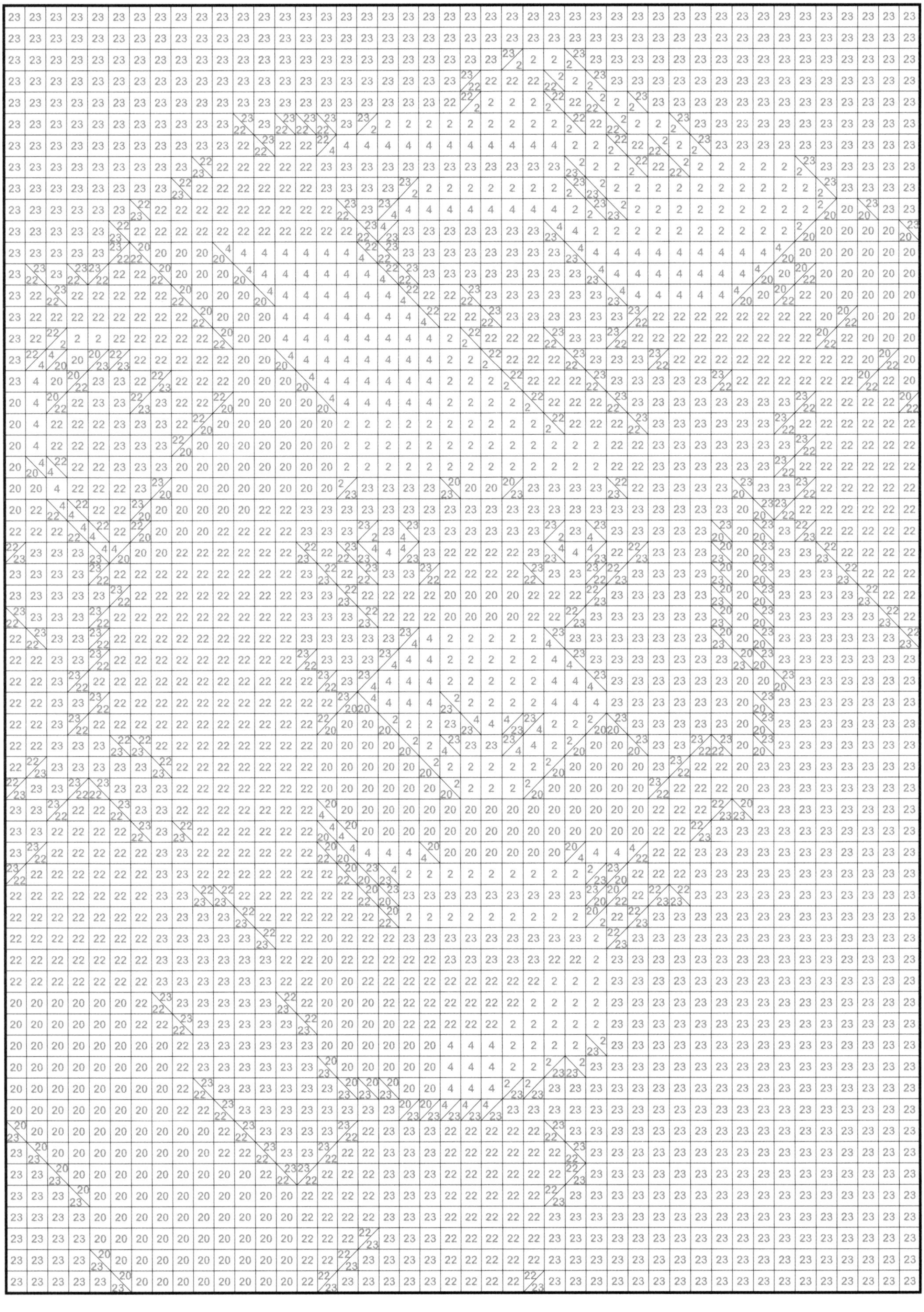

PUZZLE 84

PUZZLE 85

PUZZLE 86

PUZZLE 87

PUZZLE 88

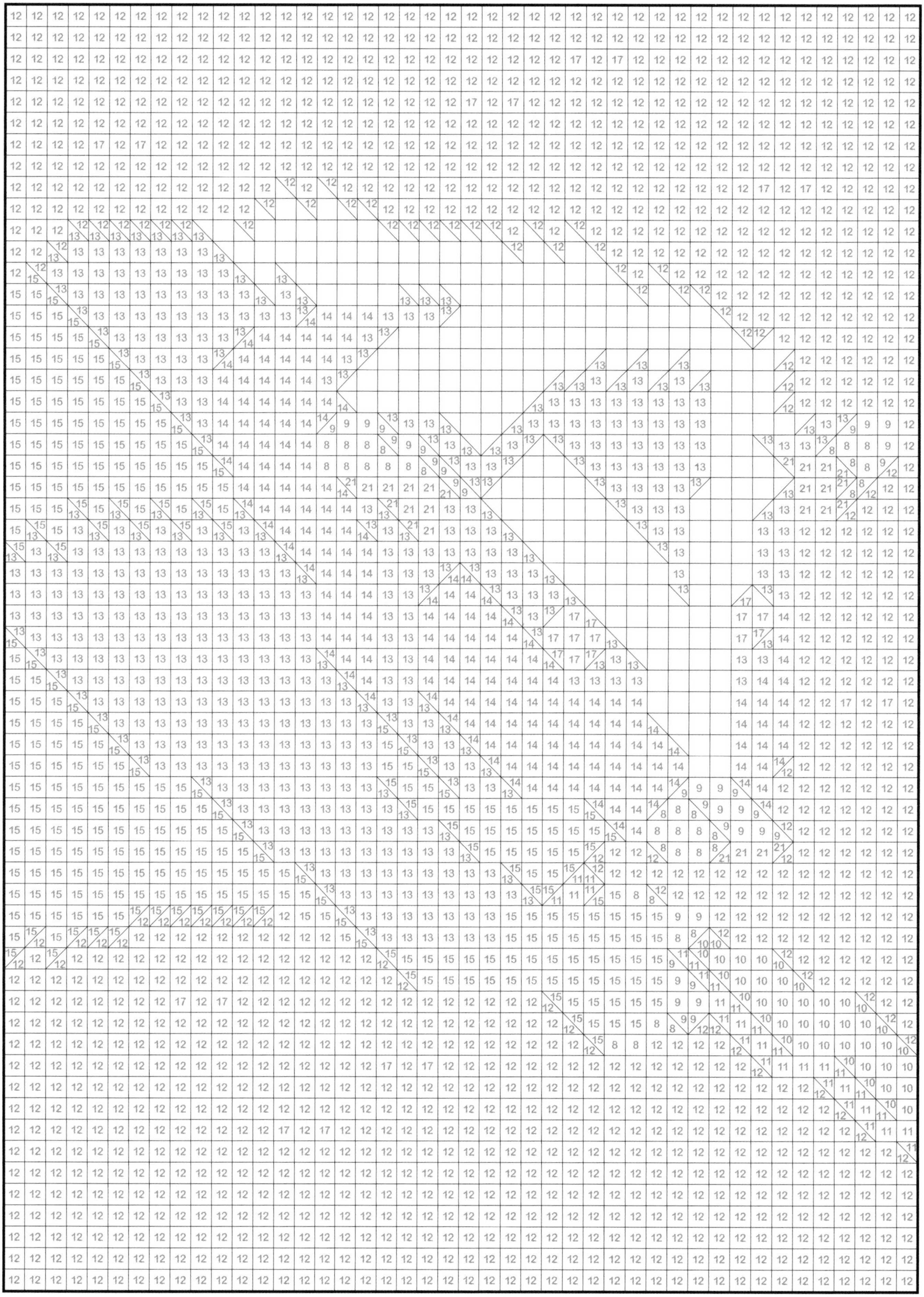

PUZZLE 89

PUZZLE 90

PUZZLE 91

PUZZLE 92

PUZZLE 93

PUZZLE 94

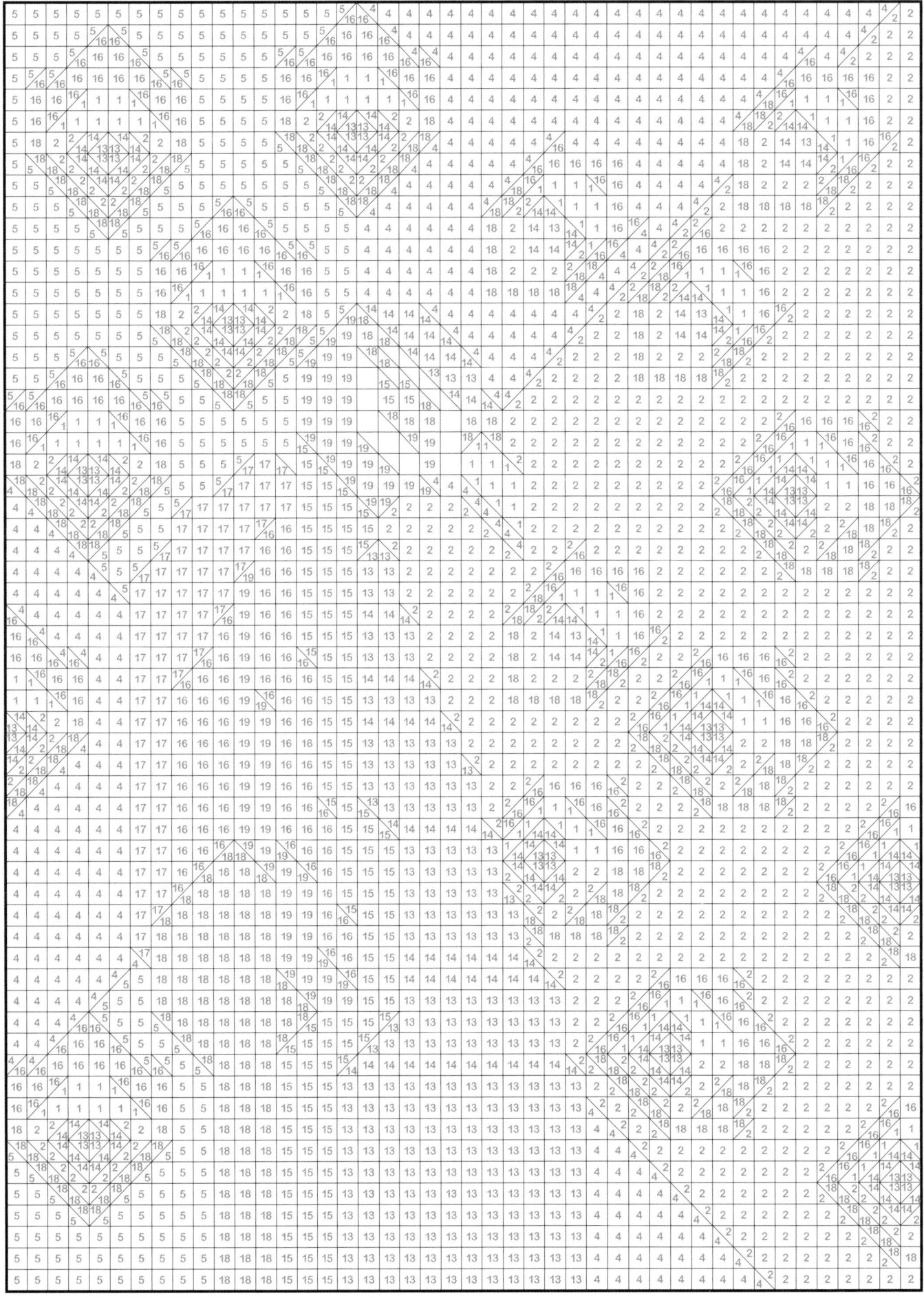

PUZZLE 95

PUZZLE 96

PUZZLE 98

PUZZLE 99

PUZZLE 100

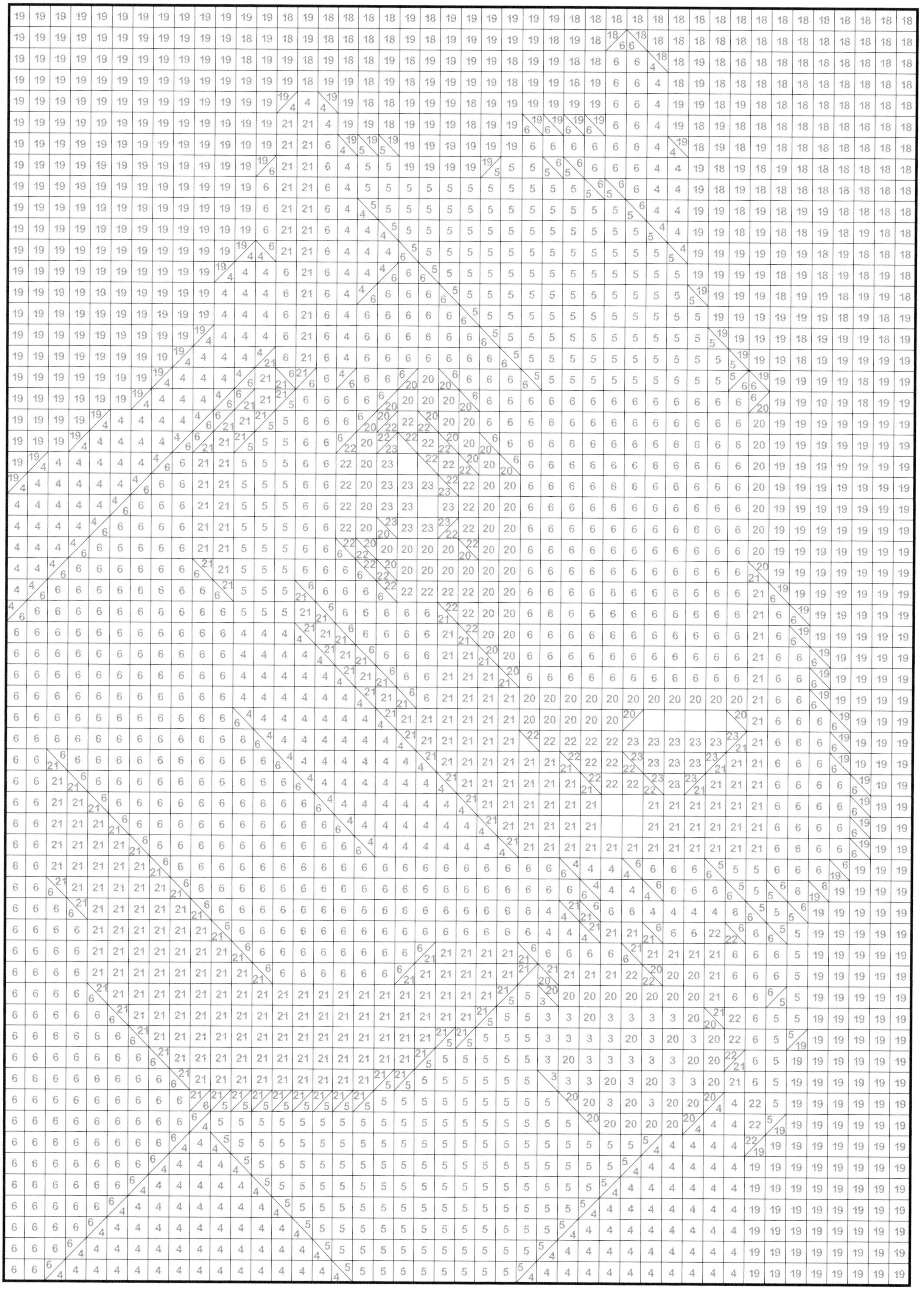

PUZZLE 102

PUZZLE 103

PUZZLE 105

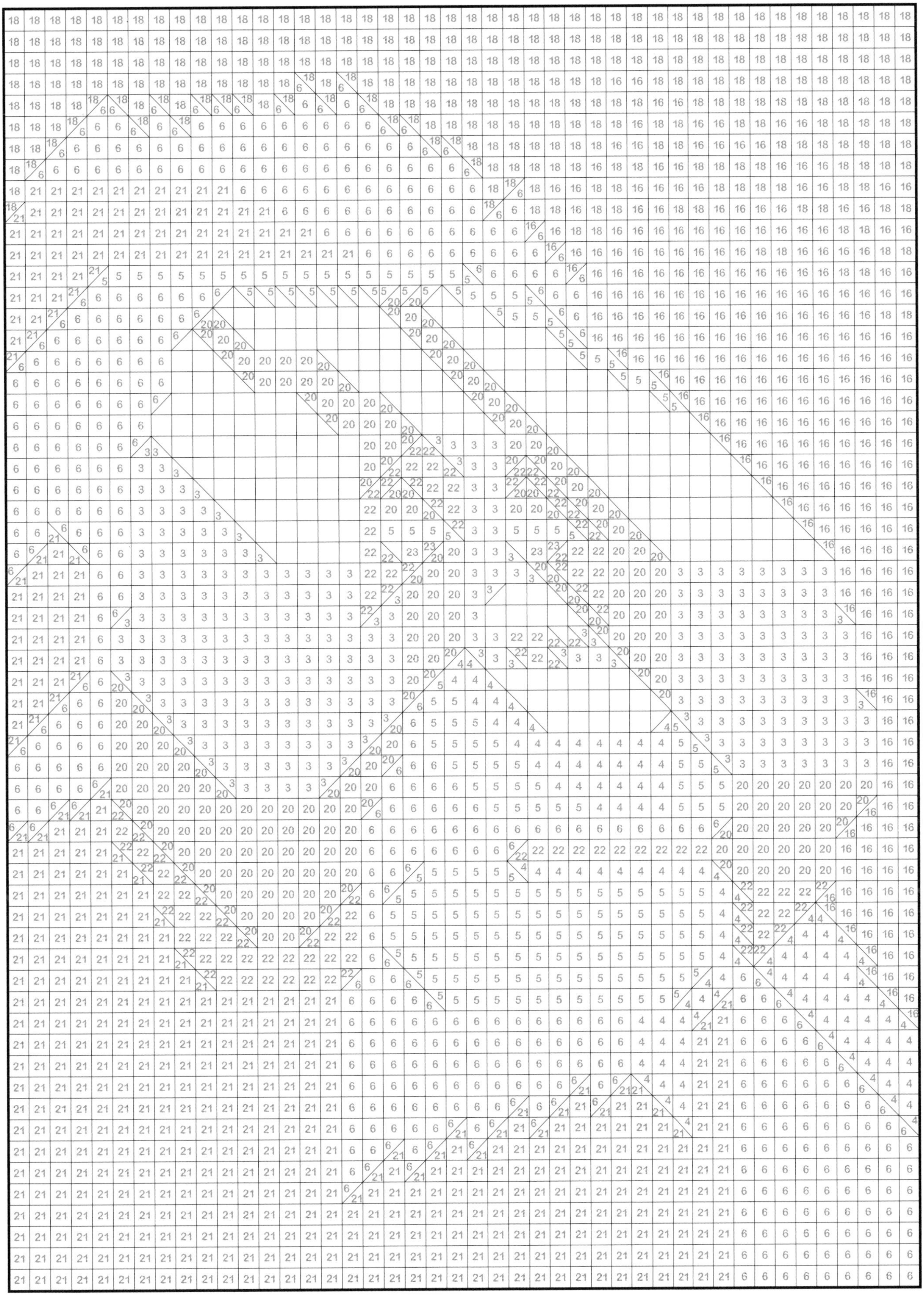

PUZZLE 106

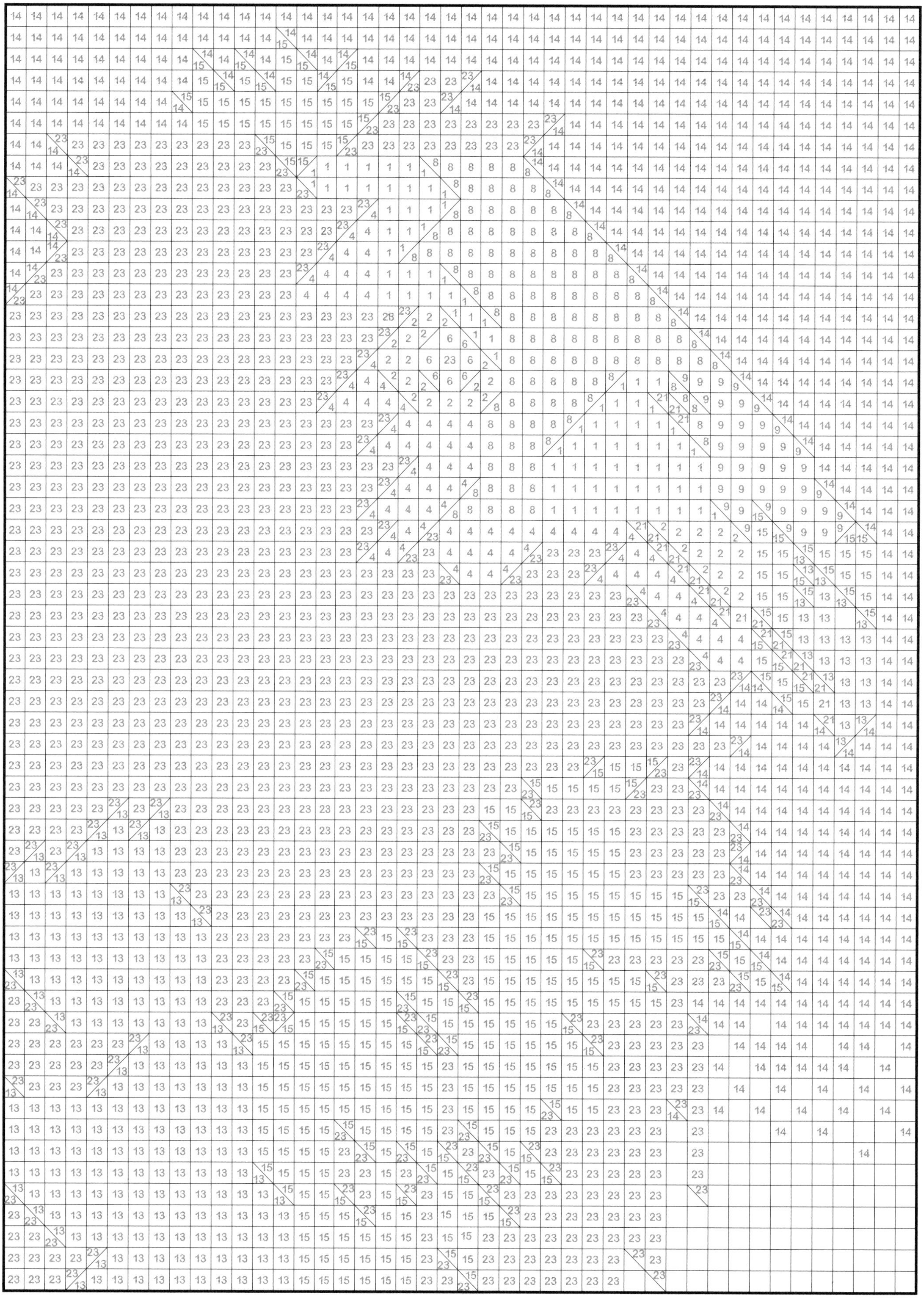

PUZZLE 108

PUZZLE 109

PUZZLE 110

PUZZLE 111

PUZZLE 112

PUZZLE 113

PUZZLE 114

PUZZLE 115

PUZZLE 116

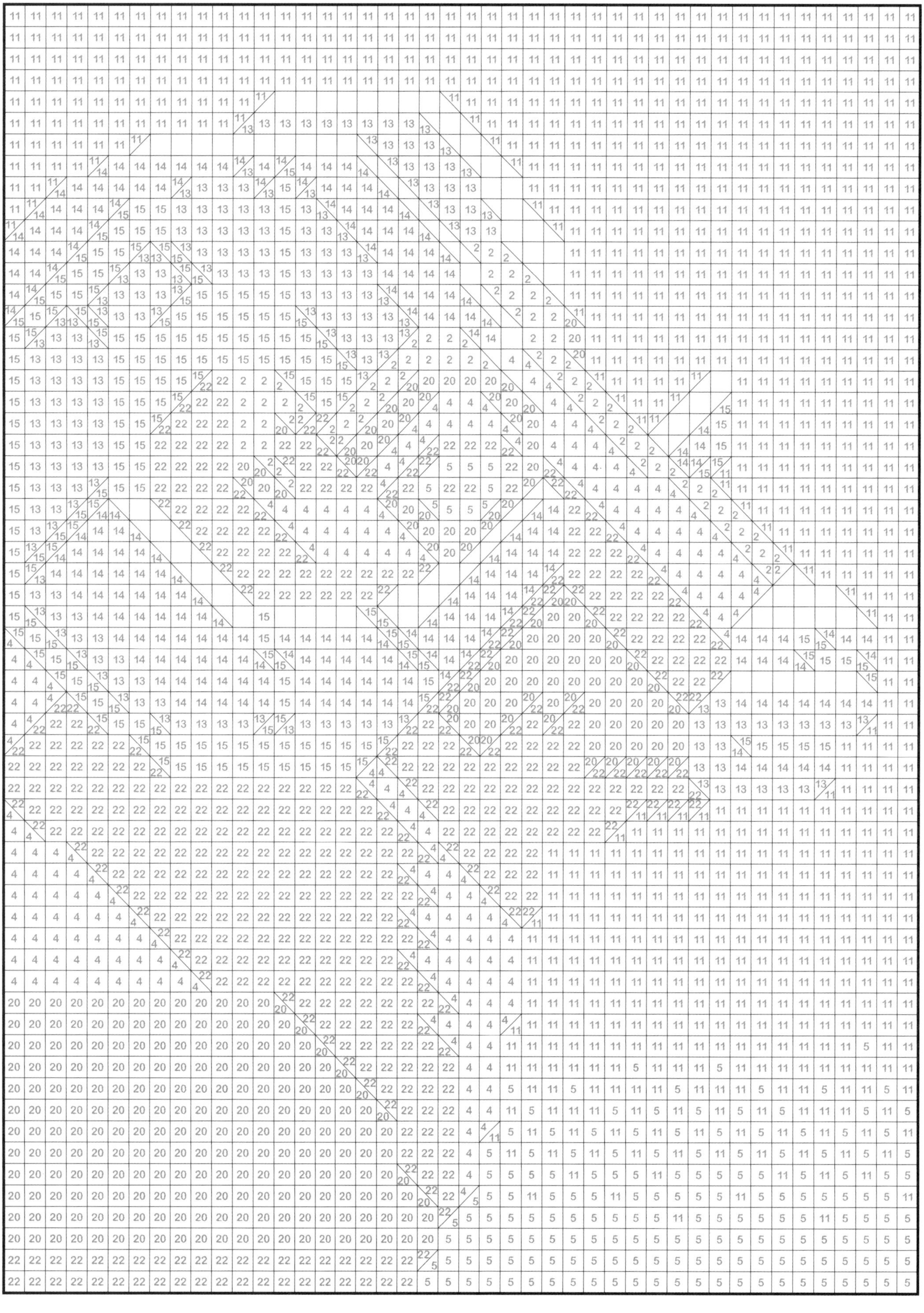

PUZZLE 117

PUZZLE 118

PUZZLE 119

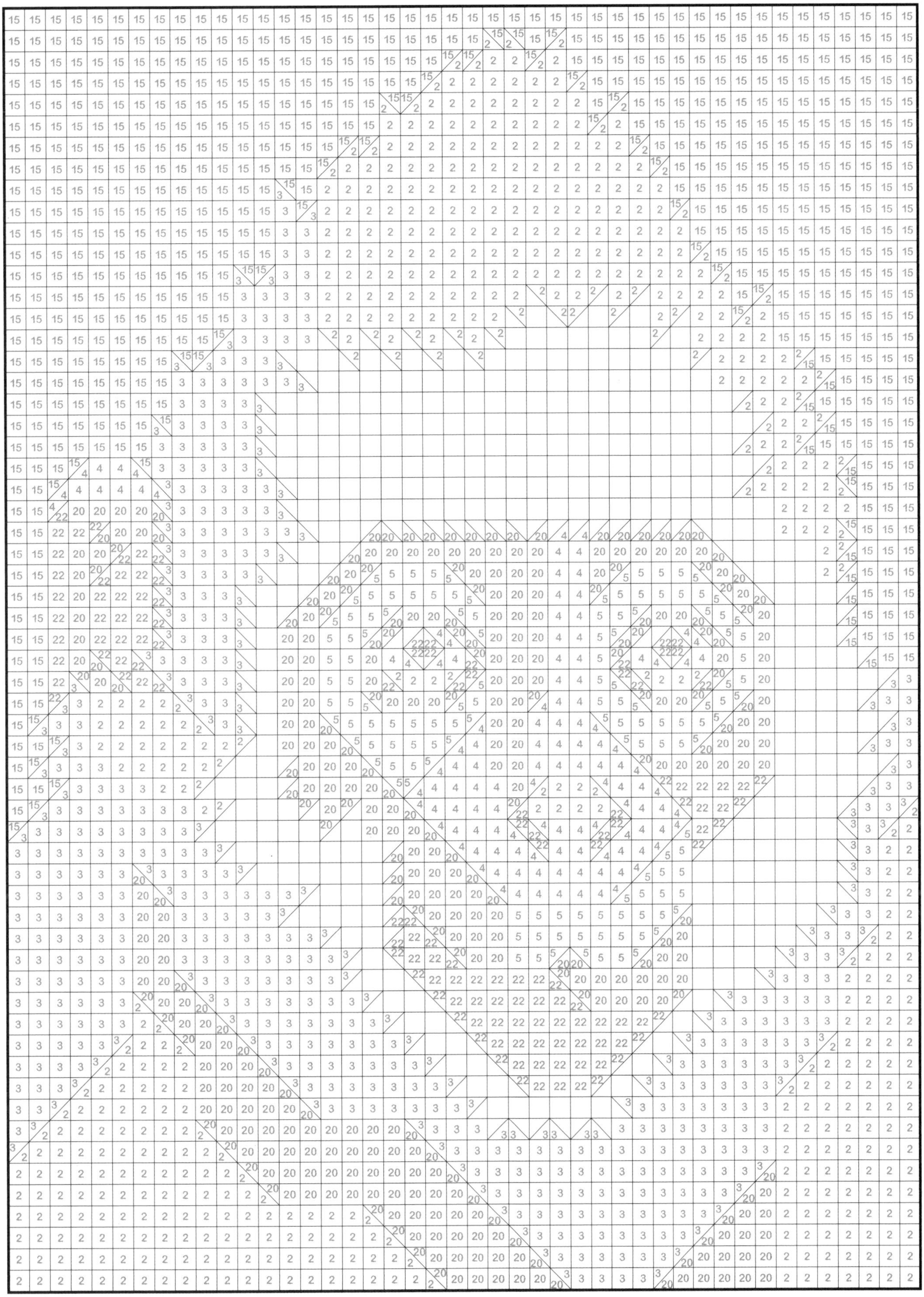

PUZZLE 120

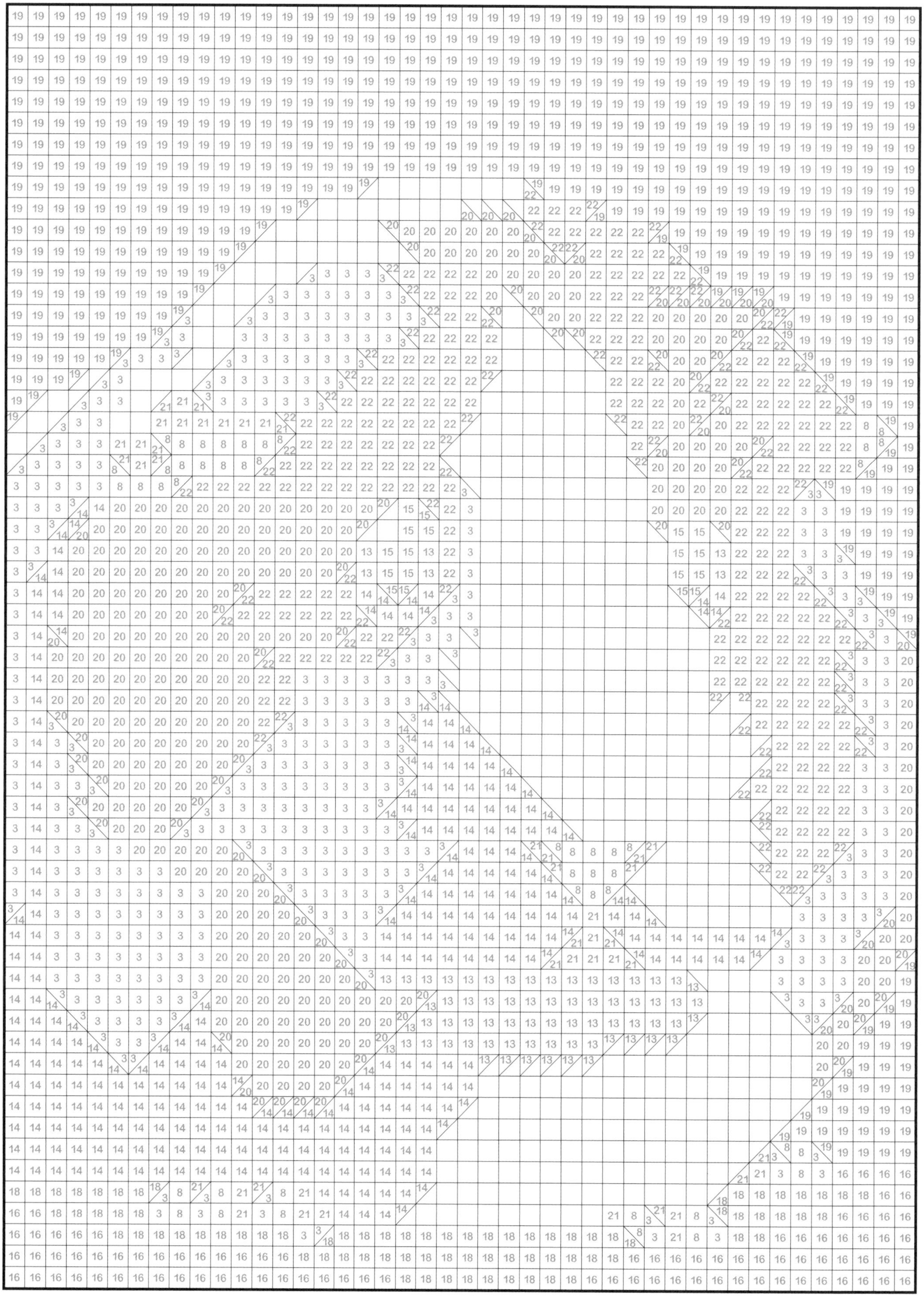

ANSWERS

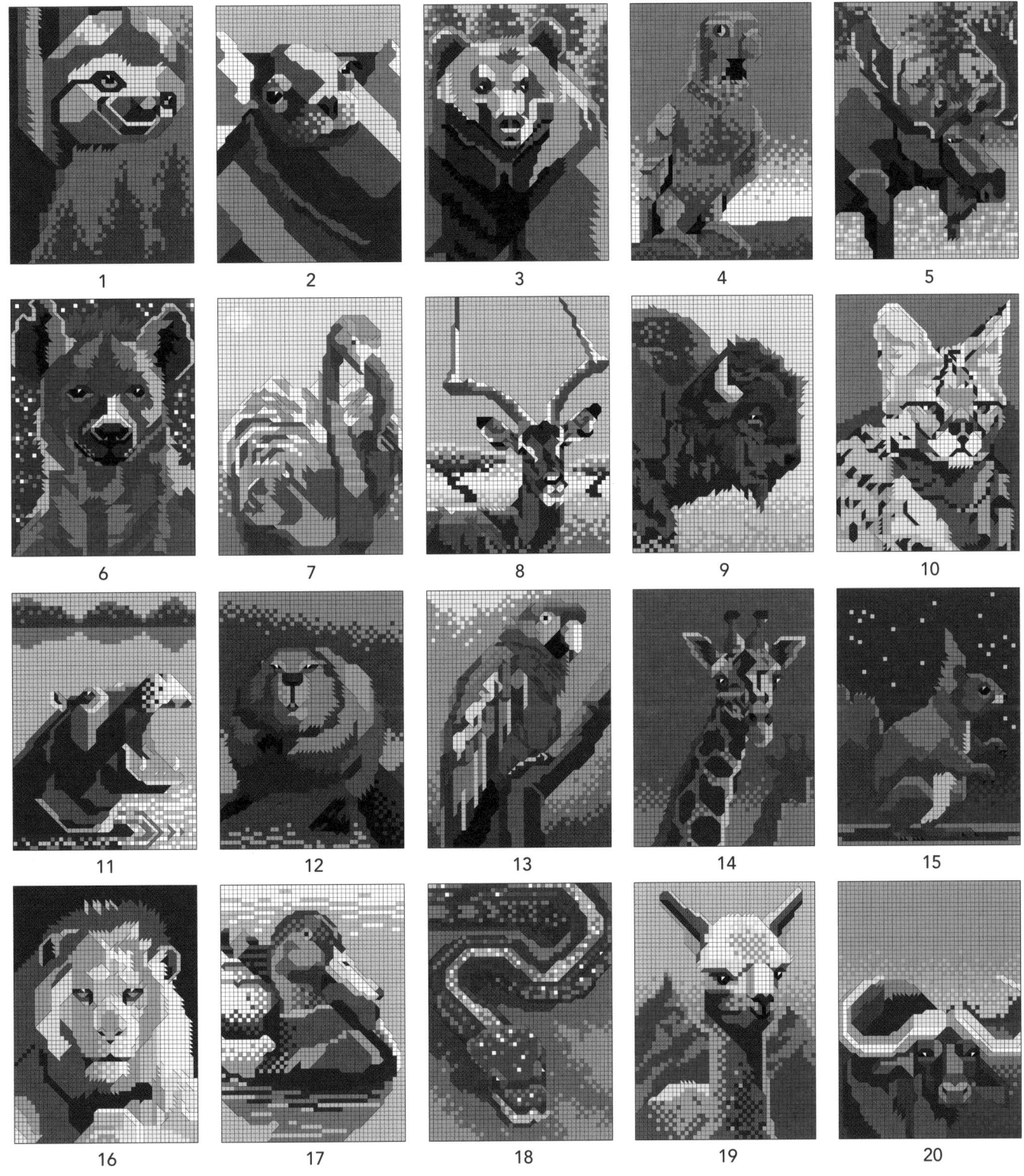

1

2

3

4

5

6

7

8

9

10

11

12

13

14

15

16

17

18

19

20

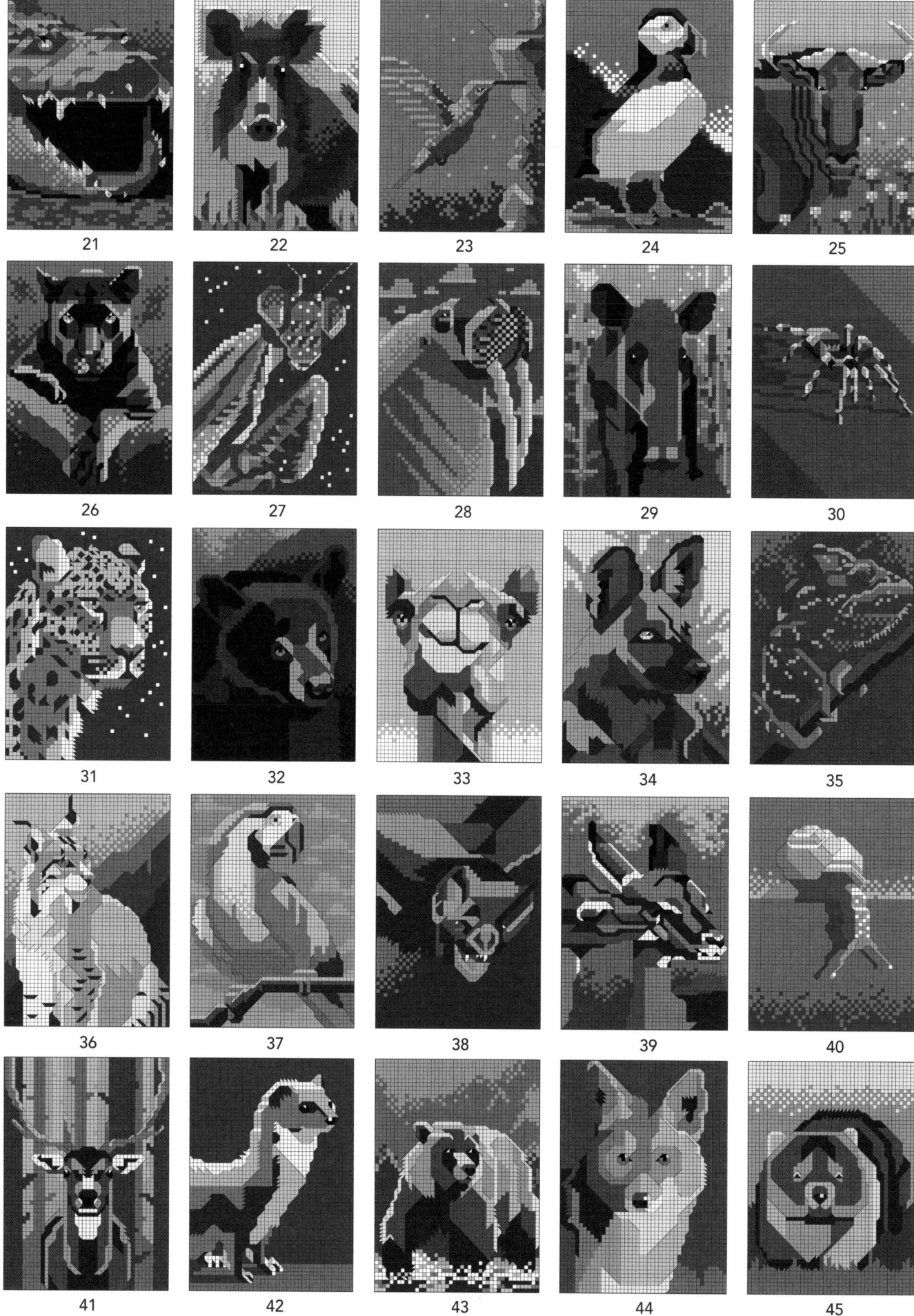

21

22

23

24

25

26

27

28

29

30

31

32

33

34

35

36

37

38

39

40

41

42

43

44

45

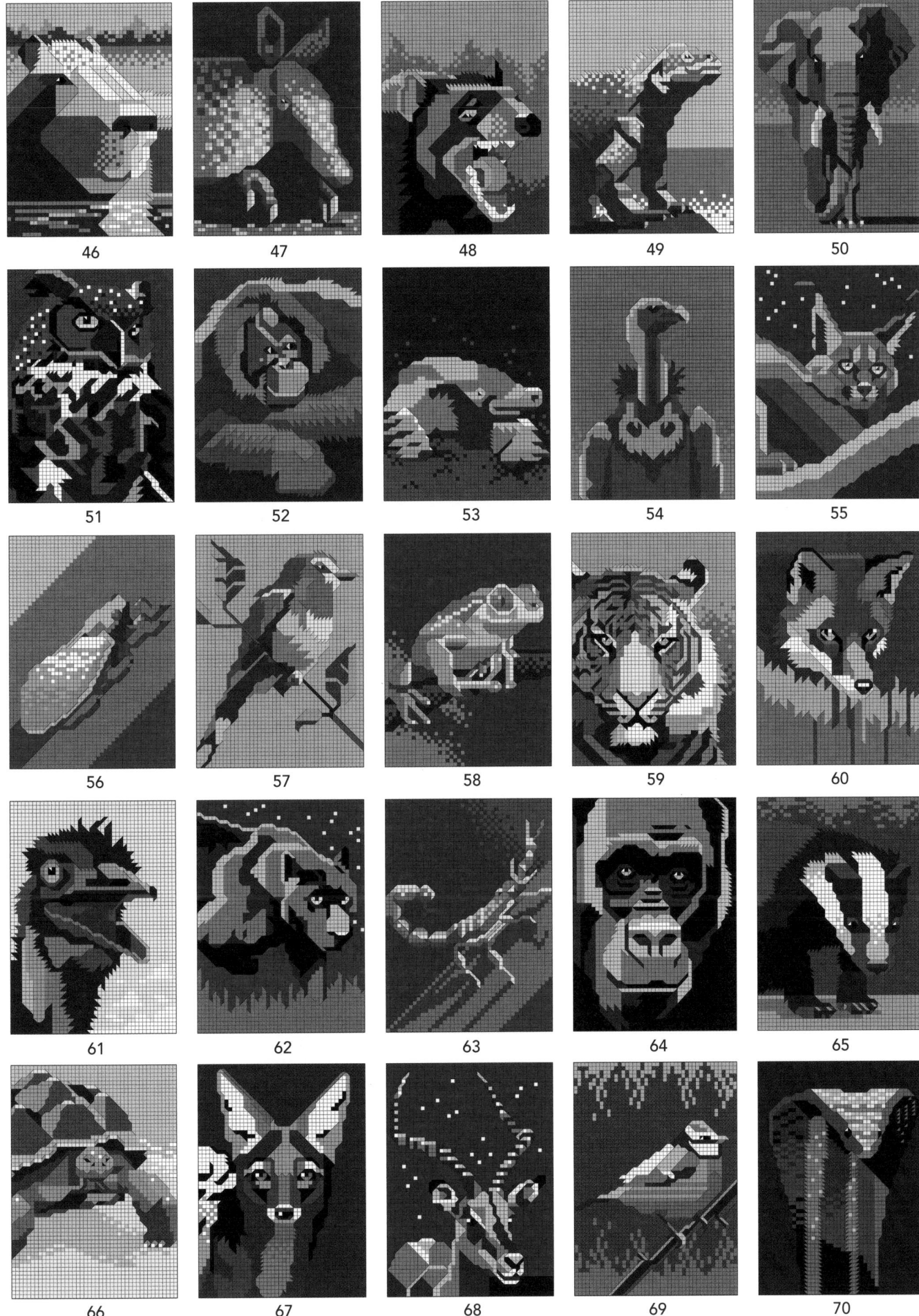

46

47

48

49

50

51

52

53

54

55

56

57

58

59

60

61

62

63

64

65

66

67

68

69

70

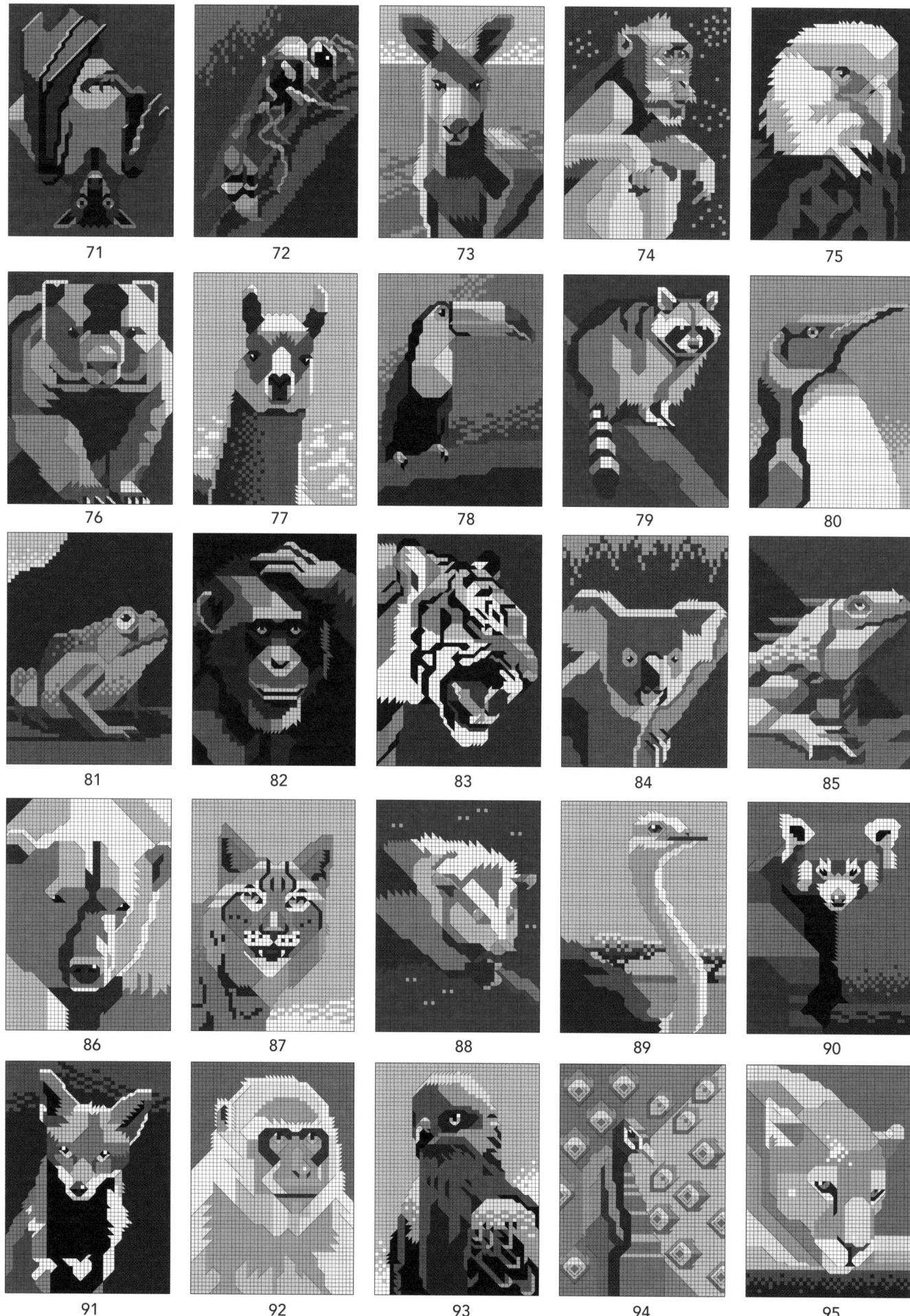

71

72

73

74

75

76

77

78

79

80

81

82

83

84

85

86

87

88

89

90

91

92

93

94

95

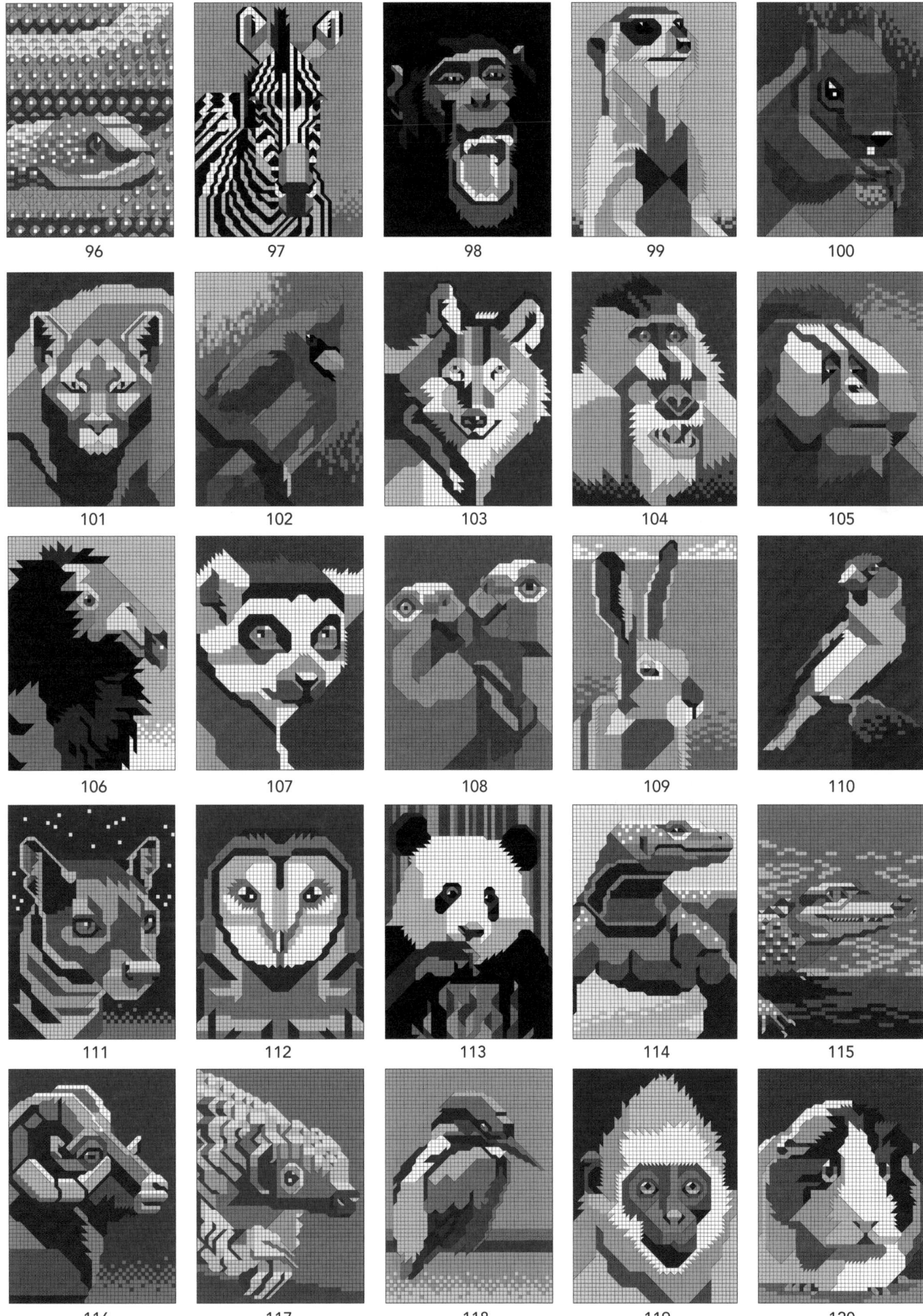

96 97 98 99 100

101 102 103 104 105

106 107 108 109 110

111 112 113 114 115

116 117 118 119 120

Get Creative 6
An imprint of Mixed Media Resources
19 West 21st Street, Suite 601
New York, NY 10010

Editor
PAMELA WISSMAN

Art Director
IRENE LEDWITH

Cover Designer
DIANE LAMPHRON

Book Designer
DANITA ALBERT

Chief Executive Officer
CAROLINE KILMER

President
ART JOINNIDES

Chairman
JAY STEIN

Manufactured in China

3 5 7 9 10 8 6 4

First Edition

DEDICATION

*For Icha and Saura, who stand
by me no matter what.*

ABOUT THE AUTHOR

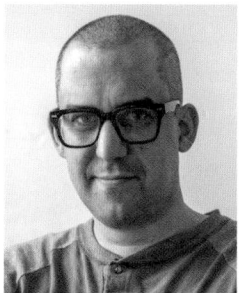

Diego Jourdan Pereira is an
author of puzzle and activity
books, including the *Giant
Book of Games and Puzzles
for Smart Kids*, *The Big Book
of Brain-Boosting Puzzles*,
Bible Power Puzzles and
Astonishing Bathroom Reader.
With a background in illustration, comic books
and graphic design, his clientele has ranged from
Dover Publications to the Topps Company.

DISCOVER MORE **MASTERPIXELS!**

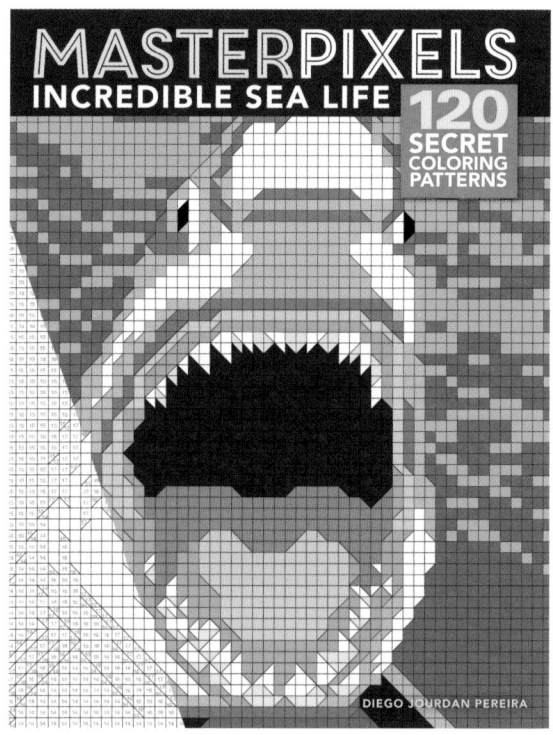